CW00860466

THE UK KETO DIET BOOK OVER 50

The Complete Guide For Sustainable Weight Loss with Quick and Healthy Recipes for Family and Friends incl. 3 Weeks Keto Challenge

OLIVIA A. PARKER

Copyright © 2021 by Olivia A. Parker

All rights reserved

All rights for this book here presented belong exclusively to the author.
Usage or reproduction of the text is forbidden and requires a clear consent of the author in
case of expectations.

ISBN - 9798524290250

TABLE OF CONTENTS

INTRODUCTION

WHAT IS A KETO DIET?

Many of us gain weight as we grow older, and some people resign themselves to accept it saying that it is "just a fact of life."

But you do not have to accept it.

Because unhealthy weight gain means declining health, and we want to stay fit and active for as long as possible!

If you have been trying to lose weight for a while you will be familiar with plans like the Atkins and Zero Carb diets, which lots of people confuse as being similar to a keto diet.

But the Keto Diet is different.

The Keto Diet can help you lose weight, reduce blood sugar levels, energise your body and mind, and drastically improve your health.

It will do so without leaving you hungry at the end of the day.

It will do so without forcing you into obsessive calorie counting.

It will do so without enforcing unrealistic limitations, until you inevitably break, and are left back at square one.

The Keto Diet is a low-carb, high-fat diet that triggers the metabolic state of ketosis. (We will get to what ketosis is in a moment...)

Fat? I thought fats were bad for you?!

Wrong!... Well, let us explain. Some fats are bad for you, but healthy fats are incredibly good for you and are the key to a healthy body and a happy life.

As we grow older it becomes more and more difficult to burn our excess fat, and while it might sound totally contradictory, eating more healthy fats can actually help you burn those stubborn fat stores for good!

There's a big difference between the healthy fat of an avocado and the unhealthy fat of crisps and processed foods - if you were looking for a diet that lets you eat saturated fats all day long we are afraid this isn't it. In fact, that isn't a diet at all.

If you want to lose weight and protect your heart health, you cannot eat lots of saturated fats. But don't worry, we have a plan that will leave you just as satisfied, more energised, and lighter than you would have been consuming unhealthy foods.

If you're still thinking that fat is exactly what you are trying to lose, how could consuming more fat possibly help? Trust us - It helps because not only is your body perfect, it is also incredibly smart.

Eating more healthy fats triggers a ketogenic state, allowing your hunger to be satisfied, and your body to begin burning fat!

Now let's talk about how we do that...

WHAT IS KETOSIS?

Ketosis is a metabolic state.

Ketosis is triggered by limiting carbohydrates, which is what your body usually breaks down first as a source of energy. Ketosis is when your body burns fat for energy instead of carbohydrates.

When your body breaks down fat it produces ketones, which become your body's energy source.

Being in a ketogenic state means your body burns fat much faster than it would if you had consumed carbohydrates.

HEALTH BENEFITS FOR THE OVER 50S?

A Keto diet can:

Aid weight loss

Reduced risk of cardiovascular illness

Energised body and mind

We all know it can be potentially dangerous to be overweight, and these risks increase as we get older.

High cholesterol, blood pressure, and blood sugar all contribute to cardiovascular disease and an unhealthy body.

Keto can reduce your blood sugars and balance your cholesterol, so you can keep your heart fit and healthy as you age and become more at risk.

Keto is also currently being studied for its potentially very positive effects on epilepsy, brain injuries, and Alzheimer's disease.

Keto speeds up your metabolism, which has been shown to decrease as we age.

Metabolism is determined by our muscle mass, and we tend to lose muscle mass as we get older.

A keto diet can help you preserve muscle.

By keeping your metabolism at a healthy speed you will continue to be able to burn excess fat and will maintain your muscle mass.

A keto diet has also been shown to stimulate hair growth, reduce arthritis pain, and can even tighten your skin - so you can look and feel younger every single day.

So yes, you can have a toned and healthy body over 50.

You can have a healthy body, heart, and mind, over 50.

This is because a keto diet rises where others fall down.

Many diets cut carbohydrates, we know this. We also know that super low-carb diets are impossible to stick to, they leave you feeling hungry, dissatisfied, and miserable.

They also leave you without energy.

As we grow older we lose what may have once seemed like endless energy reserves, and it becomes more and more important to keep our energy reserves high so that we can keep up with our busy lives, children, and even grandchildren.

The more energy we have, the more we move. Ageing can often mean slowing down, and slowing down often means ageing further. On a keto diet, you will find you have more energy than you have had in years, as your body becomes much more efficient at burning fat stores for energy.

And the more energy you have, the more you move, the more weight you lose!

A keto diet stops you from reaching for unhealthy foods that can damage your health and deplete your energy.

Healthy fats are the most satiating and satisfying things you can eat!

They leave you energised, fuller for longer, and help your body burn off your fat stores quicker than ever - because this isn't a diet you'll want to give up on.

This is a diet that will become part of your life. It won't seem like a diet at all.

Just remember to always speak to a medical professional before starting a new diet plan or weightless regime.

A ketogenic diet can also benefit older adults because it provides the nutrients that many of us lack, which alleviates symptoms we may not have even associated with our diet, and have just put down to ageing. Being deficient in nutrients like Iron, Vitamin D, and certain fats can cause problems such as; fatigue, brain fog, cognitive impairment, and increased heart disease and cancer risks, as well as problems with sight and skin.

You do not have to accept these issues as part of growing older, what you put into your body has a huge effect on your health, and you may be amazed at how more energised, alert, and healthy you feel.

As we grow older we still need to be consuming the same number of vitamins and nutrients we have always needed, but we become less able to cope with any deficiencies. We also lose some of the resilience we once had, so living on junk food and snacks as we may have in our youth is no longer something our bodies can cope with. They need higher quality fuel, and that's what keto is all about, providing your body with everything it really needs for the healthiest version of you.

WHAT FOODS SHOULD I BE EATING?

On a keto diet it is important to choose the right kinds of foods, and the right kinds of fat - otherwise you'll be creating exactly the opposite effect to what you want.

This book contains loads of healthy, delicious recipes to put you on the right track, but here are some go-to ingredients to get you started:

Meat - like beef, pork, and poultry

Fish - fatty fish such as tuna, salmon, and mackerel

Avocados - a great source of healthy fat

Eggs

Butter, Creams & Full-Fat Yoghurt*

Cheese - unprocessed with no added sweetener

Nuts

Oils - extra virgin olive oil, avocado, coconut*, sesame

Seeds - chia, flax, pumpkin

Vegetables - ONLY those with low levels of carbohydrates such as leafy greens, mushrooms, tomatoes, onions, celery, peppers, broccoli, green beans

*Yoghurt is a great source of protein and healthy fat but should be enjoyed in moderation as it does contain carbs. And make sure you aren't choosing something fat-free or sweetened.

*Coconut Oil should be used in moderation as it is saturated fat.

WHAT FOODS SHOULD I AVOID?

There are 3 factors you need to consider:

Carbohydrates

Sugar

Unhealthy Fats

Eating carbohydrates will knock you right out of ketosis, and force you to try and reach the metabolic state the next day.

Losing a day like this can happen now and again - it's okay - but to really achieve an alteration in health and weight you will want to maintain ketosis as much as possible.

The problem is lots of people don't actually realise how much of our common western foods contain high levels of carbohydrates - so much of our fruit and veg is very high-carb!

So, reduce the intake of carbohydrates as much as possible.

Sugar also catches lots of people out. This is because when you eat sugar, the body can burn that for fuel instead, so it will not burn your fat reserves as we want it to.

And finally, unhealthy fats.

We mentioned this earlier, but you must consider the kinds of fat that you put in your body. There are healthy fats, which can actually improve your heart health, and there are bad, saturated fats, which can clog your arteries, damage your organs, and put a serious strain on your body.

So, as a general guideline, try to avoid foods like:

Root vegetables and high-carb vegetables - like potato and carrots

Grains - wheat products, bread, pasta, rice

Fruit - small portions of berries being the exception

Beans, legumes, and lentils

Sugar Foods & Beverages - stay away from fizzy drinks, bakery items, sweets, etc

Processed foods - including processed sugars, dairy and meat

So-called "sugar-free" or "fat-free" diet items

Unhealthy fats - foods high in saturated fats like vegetable oil, milk, lard

Overly fatty meats - such as lamb

PLANNING

We will run the risk of sounding like a broken record and emphasise repeatedly that planning is so important.

Success doesn't just happen, and if you think you can see people crushing their weight loss goals and healthy eating plans, you should take a look inside their lives. They are making it look easy, and it is easy because they plan.

The only reason anyone should fail at this diet is if they expect their lives to magically become free, and easy, and for it to revolve around you and your eating habits.

It won't.

You must fit your eating plan into your lifestyle, not the other way around.

That isn't to say that you cannot adjust your life by making healthier choices, like swapping family pizza night for family Keto MasterChef night or opting for a walk and a chat rather than a sit-down and chat. Little things can make a big difference.

But the times you will fall out of ketosis will be the times you have no other options, like having no ingredients in, or waiting too long before a meal until you crack.

Be kind to yourself, and plan ahead.

<u>The 3 Week Keto Challenge</u>

At the end of this book, you will find three weeks' worth of guidance and menus to help you as your start your keto journey.

The guide is easy to follow and every day you will receive an extra BONUS recipe for a ketogenic meal for either breakfast, lunch, or dinner!

That's 21 New Recipes to try!

Keto Tips & Tricks

No beating yourself up if you don't always get it right straight away, undertaking a new diet plan is a big change and you're allowed to have a few off days!

A problem shared is a problem halved. Do you have friends or family who also want to lose weight and improve their health? Why not undertake the challenge together?

Remove the temptations. The Keto Diet is satisfying and delicious - but we're only human! Of course, you will get occasional cravings for things you've always been allowed to have before. Simple solution - don't have them in the house! If you've squirrelled away a pack of biscuits "just in case", that "just in case" moment will arrive sooner and more often than you anticipate, trust us. Fill your home with things you can have, and always have a meal prepared in the fridge - which brings us to our next point...

Don't leave yourself stuck. We can all start the day with the best intentions, but they can quickly go out the window after a long day when hunger pangs start hitting. If you arrive home to find nothing keto to eat, of course, you're going to grab whatever you find! Do yourself a favour and plan your meal preparations and shopping trips around your busy lifestyle, arriving home to something you can whip up in 15 minutes will be much more manageable after those hectic days.

Listen to your body. Keto is a satisfying diet! It can literally reduce hunger, but you won't feel the effects of this if you're not listening to what your body is telling you and feeding it anyway. We are operating by society's clock, and forcing our bodies into feeding and fasting when convenient for us and our lifestyle. It's time to get back in tune. This can be hard when work and social conventions demand certain things of us but try to listen to what your body really needs. Are you hungry yet or just eating because everyone else is? Are you actually thirsty, have you had enough water today? Do you need to eat that much, or are you already full and can perhaps save the rest for later? All these choices are about listening to what your body really needs.

Keto responsibly. Changing your diet means literally changing what you put into your body. Now is a perfect time to consider what ingredients, portions, and nutrients actually do to your body. Your body is the only one you're going to get; this diet should help you to really consider how you fuel it and what effect that has on the inside as well as the outside. Speak to your doctor or nutritionist about the impact of a healthy eating plan, and the choices you want to make to support your future.

The following recipes for breakfast, lunch, and dinner will help you make informed and balanced choices that will help you follow a ketogenic diet and achieve ketosis. If you're still in need of guidance or are just looking for a good way to kick off your plan, turn to the 3 Week Keto Challenge and begin your journey to a healthier body.

Olivia A. Parker

BREAKFAST

Start your day right! Kick-off ketosis with these tasty breakfast recipes that will leave you feeling energised, motivated, and fuller for longer! All the recipes are easy to follow and can be altered to suit however many portions you are serving.

Many recipes, like the Breakfast Muffins and Granola, can be prepared in large batches and stored so that you know you have a quick and easy breakfast waiting for you on those hectic mornings. In contrast, meals like the Steak, Avocado & Egg Tower take a little longer to prepare, so you may want to save those for a morning you are not rushing out the door.

The most important thing is – do NOT skip breakfast.

You are breaking the fast you have been in since your evening meal several hours and a goodnight's sleep later. Let your body begin its work and fuel it for the day ahead by providing it with what it needs. Your body cannot become a lean fat-burning machine if it is worried about when its next meal will come.

PANCAKES

A diet that includes pancakes – who'd have thought it!

These delicious and satisfying pancakes will keep you full well into lunch-time and are the perfect way to begin a ketogenic day. And the best part is that they are so easy to make, you can have a batch of hot pancakes whipped up for the whole family in no time.

SERVES: 5 (2 PANCAKES PER SERVING)
PREPARATION TIME: 15 MINS
NUTRITION: KCALS 225
NET CARBOHYDRATES 6.6G
FIBRE 2G
FAT 18G
PROTEIN 9.2G

INGREDIENTS:

- ◆ 4 Eggs
- ◆ 65g of Almond Flour
- ◆ 100g of Soft Cream Cheese
- ◆ 1 drop of Vanilla Extract
- ◆ 200g of Strawberries
- ◆ Butter

Olivia A. Parker

HOW TO PREPARE:

1 Start by hulling and halving your strawberries so that they are ready to be served, and set to one side.

2 Weigh out your almond flour and soft cream cheese, then add them into a mixing bowl.

3 Take your eggs and whisk them in a small bowl or jug. Add your whisked eggs and vanilla essence into the mixing bowl, now whisk together all ingredients until you have a smooth batter.

4 Place a non-stick pan over medium heat and allow to heat up, then add a knob of butter. Allow the butter to melt and cover the surface of the pan.

5 Pour a small dollop of the mixture into the centre of the pan, it should be about 3 to 4 tablespoons worth – you can measure this out beforehand and then add to the pan if it is easier.

6 Allow the first side to cook for approximately 2 minutes. It should not burn in this time, but check the first pancake as you may need to reduce your heat.

7 Flip your pancake! Everyone's favourite part – if you aren't a seasoned pancake flipper you can always use a spatula.

8 Allow two more minutes on the second side, then serve immediately with a knob of butter and a handful of strawberries. A simple easy breakfast everyone will love!

KETO GRANOLA

Who says you can't still enjoy a tasty bowl of Granola in the morning?

This quick and delicious recipe can provide you with breakfast for the entire week! Just store it in an airtight container in a cool dry place and serve up with milk or yoghurt of your choice!

SERVES: 8
PREPARATION TIME: 15 MINS
NUTRITION: KCALS 452
NET CARBOHYDRATES 12G
FIBRE 7.1G
FAT 43.25G
PROTEIN 11.2G

INGREDIENTS:

- 1 Egg White
- 150g of Almonds
- 150g of Walnuts
- 150g of Pecans
- 3 tbsp of Flax Seeds
- 2 tbsp of Sesame Seeds
- 2 tsp of Ground Cinnamon
- 2 tbsp of Coconut Oil
- 1 tbsp of Chia Seeds
- Half a tsp of Salt
- 1 drop of Vanilla Extract

HOW TO PREPARE:

1 First, set your oven to preheat at 150° Celsius.

2 Measure out and chop all of the whole nuts into little pieces, and place them in a large bowl.

3 Add the flax seeds, chia seeds, sesame seeds, salt, and cinnamon into the mixing bowl, and then mix all the ingredients together.

4 Whisk the egg white until nice and frothy, then stir in one drop of vanilla essence. Pour into the mixing bowl and stir to coat the granola.

5 Melt the coconut oil and add to the mixing bowl, then stir well.

6 Take a baking tray and cover with a sheet of greaseproof baking paper, then pour your granola mixture onto the paper.

7 Spread out evenly and then bake in the oven for 15 minutes. Remover the tray and give the mixture a light stir, before returning to the oven and baking for another 10 minutes, or until golden brown.

8 Let the granola cool before placing it in an airtight container for storing, or straight into your bowl if you're ready for breakfast!

SEA - SAUSAGE, EGG & AVOCADO TOWER

The SEA - Three classic keto ingredients towered together into one tasty breakfast that you and your whole family will love. Low in carbs and high in good fat and protein, this indulgent meal is perfect for a Sunday morning breakfast you will want to savour.

SERVES: 1
PREPARATION TIME:15 MINS
NUTRITION: KCALS 578
NET CARBOHYDRATES 11G
FIBRE 7G
FAT 47G
PROTEIN 29G

INGREDIENTS:

♦ 2 Large Eggs
♦ 1 Slice of Cheese
♦ 1 Pork Sausage Patty
♦ 2 tsp of Double Cream
♦ 1 tsp of Butter
♦ Half an Avocado
♦ Salt & Pepper to taste

HOW TO PREPARE:

1 Firstly, take half an avocado and slice it into fine strips. Set to one side so that it is ready to be fanned out on top of your tower once the other ingredients are cooked.

2 Break your eggs into a small bowl and add in the double cream, then whisk everything together thoroughly. Season with salt and pepper if desired.

3 Heat a non-stick pan over medium heat before placing your sausage patty in the pan and cooking both sides through, they should be nicely browned and be sure to check that the meat is properly cooked.

4 Once the patty is done place it on your plate and top with a slice of cheese, this will allow it to melt.

5 Melt your butter in a non-stick pan, then pour the egg mixture slowly into the centre of the pan.

6 Allow the egg to cook until it is taking on a more solid shape before folding the sides into the centre so that you have a thicker and more square shape.

7 Remove the egg from the pan and place it on top of the sausage patty and melted cheese, then top the egg with the fanned slices of avocado.

8 Your SEA tower is ready, enjoy your quick and easy keto breakfast.

RASPBERRY & VANILLA MUFFINS

Cake for breakfast? Yes please! These scrumptious little muffins are perfect for grabbing on the go, so you can still hit your keto targets while rushing to start your day. They're simple, delicious, and can be stored throughout the week so you know you've got tomorrow's breakfast good to go.

SERVES: 6 (2 MUFFINS PER SERVING)
PREPARATION TIME: 50 MINS
NUTRITION: KCALS 472
NET CARBOHYDRATES 16G
FIBRE 4G
FAT 40G
PROTEIN 13G

INGREDIENTS:

- 3 Large Eggs
- 280g of Almond Flour
- 80g of Melted Butter
- 80g of Fresh Raspberries
- 80ml of Unsweetened Almond Milk
- 65g of Keto-Friendly Sugar
- Half a tbsp of Baking Powder
- Half a tsp of Baking Soda
- Half a tsp of Salt
- 1 drop of Vanilla Extract

HOW TO PREPARE:

1 Preheat your oven to 170° Celsius. Now take your muffin tray and line the bases with muffin or cupcake cases. (This recipe is for twelve muffins, but you can always reduce the quantities if you have a smaller muffin tray - or make more batches!)

2 Whisk your eggs in a bowl and add in the drop of vanilla extract. Pour in the melted butter and almond milk and stir together all liquid ingredients.

3 Place the almond flour, keto-friendly sugar, baking powder, baking soda, and salt into a mixing bowl.

4 Pour about a quarter of the liquid into the mixing bowl and whisk together. Continue this action until all the liquid is well whisked and you are left with a smooth muffin batter.

5 Take the raspberries and gently fold them into the batter until they are well distributed.

6 Carefully scoop the batter into the muffin cases and place the tray into the oven.

7 Allow the muffins to cook for approximately 20 mins, or until they are a light golden brown and cooked through - test the centre of the muffins by placing a toothpick into the middle and checking to see if it comes out clean.

8 Enjoy your delicious little breakfast muffins!

BERRY & AVOCADO SMOOTHIE

A perfect blend of fibre and healthy fat, this go-to Breakfast Smoothie is quick, delicious and highly nutritious. This breakfast is perfect for a busy morning and is ideal for fitting your keto targets around your lifestyle. It is also a super flexible recipe, so feel free to mix and match the berries you want to use,

SERVES:
PREPARATION TIME: 2 MINS
NUTRITION: KCALS 415
NET CARBOHYDRATES 30G
FIBRE 18G
FAT 28G
PROTEIN 13G

INGREDIENTS:

◆ Frozen Berries i.e, Strawberries, Blueberries, Blackberries, Red Currants etc.

◆ Half an Avocado

◆ 30g of Spinach

◆ 1 tbsp of Hemp Seeds

◆ 1 tbsp Chia Seeds

◆ 250ml of Water

HOW TO PREPARE:

1 This one is easy. Simply add all of your ingredients into a blender - and blend!

2 You can even add some ice if you want to bulk up the texture a bit.

3 Enjoy your satisfying keto smoothie!

GREEN EGGS

Do you like Green Eggs and Ham?... Well, not ham, but these scrumptious Green Eggs are a fun and tasty treat to kick off your morning with a little bit of spice and a lot of nutrition. This recipe is easy to double up on quantities, so you can serve it up to the whole family, and is a delicious way of eating all those healthy leafy greens.

SERVES: 1
PREPARATION TIME: 15 MINS
NUTRITION: KCALS 411
NET CARBOHYDRATES 26G
FIBRE 5G
FAT 27G
PROTEIN 20G

INGREDIENTS:

- ♦ 2 Large Eggs
- ♦ 1 tbsp of Olive Oil
- ♦ 1 tbsp of Greek Yogurt
- ♦ 1 Trimmed Leek
- ♦ 1 Handful of Kale
- ♦ 1 Handful of Spinach
- ♦ 1 Garlic Clove
- ♦ 1 tsp of Chilli Flakes
- ♦ Pinch of Salt
- ♦ Pinch of Coriander to garnish

HOW TO PREPARE:

1 Slice the garlic clove and trim the leek.

2 Place a non-stick pan over medium heat and add the olive oil. Sauté the leek and kale with a pinch of salt until tender.

3 Add the garlic and chilli flakes and cook for one minute.

4 Place the spinach into the pan and reduce the heat slightly. Stir everything together until the spinach has wilted.

5 Use a spoon to create two spaces in the mixture big enough to fry the eggs in, then add a little olive oil to each space.

6 Break an egg into each space and then allow to fry until the white is firm and the yolk is still slightly runny.

7 Carefully scoop the contents of the pan onto a plate, then top the green mixture with a dollop of Greek yoghurt.

8 Season with salt and pepper to taste.

9 Dig into your super healthy, super green, super keto breakfast!

SPICY EGG ROLL

A simple and delicious way to enjoy your eggs in the morning. This recipe replaces the traditional tortilla wrap with a finely spread omelette, to cut the carbs and up the healthy fats, and you'll find it's all the more filling for it. You can mix it up and create this roll with bacon & avocado, or even add cheese for extra flavour.

SERVES: 1
PREPARATION TIME: 15
NUTRITION: KCALS 307
NET CARBOHYDRATES 10G
FIBRE 3G
FAT 24G
PROTEIN 14G

INGREDIENTS:

- ♦ 2 Large Eggs
- ♦ 1 tbsp of Olive Oil
- ♦ 2 tbsp of Tomato Salsa (with no added sugar)
- ♦ Half a Red Pepper
- ♦ Half a Yellow Pepper
- ♦ Coriander to garnish

HOW TO PREPARE:

1 Whisk the eggs in a small bowl with a tablespoon of water.

2 Chop your pepper halves into fine bite-sized slices.

3 Heat a non-stick pan over medium heat and add half the olive oil.

4 Fry peppers until soft, then tip into a bowl and set to one side.

5 Add the remainder of the oil to the pan and allow it to heat up before reducing the heat slightly and pouring in the egg mixture.

6 Tilt the pan back and forth to ensure the entire base of the pan is covered with egg and that it is equally distributed. Cook until the egg has set.

7 Carefully tip the egg out onto a plate, ensuring it doesn't fold into itself.

8 Spoon the salsa onto the flat egg base and spread.

9 Add the peppers to the salsa and spread out, then roll the egg base up like you would a crepe, encasing all the salsa and peppers inside.

10 Serve immediately with coriander to garnish.

LUNCH

After starting your day with a nourishing keto breakfast, build on your progress by having one of our delicious and nutritious keto lunches.

These quick and easy recipes can be prepared and refrigerated, so you can grab them on the go, or serve them up to your entire family to enjoy your lunch together.

We often find that lunch is when lots of people fall down, after all, if you haven't taken anything out with you on a busy day, of course, you will want to grab whatever you can find.

It is also when people can find themselves lulling in energy, and dragging their feet into the afternoon without the proper energy required to function. The mistake so many people make is that they try to energise the body with the wrong kind of food. The carb-coma is real and is the reason why so many of us mention the thought of an afternoon nap by 2pm.

It doesn't have to be this way. With our ketogenic lunches, you will not only beat the cravings but also step into the afternoon feeling revived and energised, powering through until dinner time.

MUSHROOM RISOTTO

Creamy, delicious mushroom risotto that keeps you in ketosis? Yes, please! You may have thought that something as traditional carb-heavy as a risotto would be a thing of the past, but you don't have to miss out on a classic and comforting dish on this diet plan. This mushroom risotto, prepared with mushrooms and cauliflower rice, is a healthy and filling lunch that you can either make and refrigerate for the week or serve up immediately to your family and friends.

SERVES: 4
PREPARATION TIME: 15
NUTRITION: KCALS 407
NET CARBOHYDRATES 22G
FIBRE (8G)
FAT 42G
PROTEIN 16G

INGREDIENTS:

- 3 tbsp of Coconut Oil
- 800g of Riced Cauliflower (approx. 2 medium cauliflowers)
- 400g of White Mushrooms
- 400g of Chestnut Mushrooms
- 1 White Onion
- 60ml of Vegetable Stock
- 4 tbsp of Cashew or Almond Butter
- 2 cloves of Garlic
- 60g of Parmesan Cheese
- Basil
- Salt / Pepper to season

Olivia A. Parker

HOW TO PREPARE:

1. First, slice all your mushrooms and set them to one side.

2. Then dice your onion and finely chop your garlic, these should also be set to one side, but separate from the mushrooms.

3. Now place your cauliflower in a food processor or blender and process until you achieve a light rice-like texture, with no large lumps.

4. Place your large pan over medium heat and warm two-thirds of your coconut oil, then add the mushrooms and allow to cook through for a few minutes. They should be tender but not too limp. Then remove the mushrooms and the cooking juices from the pan, and place them in a small bowl until required.

5. Heat your remaining coconut oil then add your onions to the pan. Allow the onions to brown slightly before reducing the heat and adding in your garlic. Cook for 2 minutes.

6. Place all of your cauliflower rice into the pan and give the mixture a good stir until the rice is coated in the oil.

7. Now pour the vegetable stock into the pan and simmer over medium heat. Stir frequently and allow to cook for 5 minutes until the cauliflower has absorbed the stock.

8. Remove the pan from the heat but do not allow it to cool. Add the nut butter, parmesan, and basil to the pan, then pour in your mushrooms and cooking juices from earlier. Give the entire mixture a good stir.

9. Serve immediately and enjoy with salt and black pepper to taste.

AVOCADO & COURGETTE SPAGHETTI

With this easy lunchtime, recipe carb cravings for a big bowl of pasta are a thing of the past. Courgetti Spaghetti is guaranteed to be your new go-to carb replacement. This lunch is perfect for packing up and taking with you on a busy day - it is light and refreshing but still satisfying enough to stave off that lunchtime hunger. You can even bulk up on the quantities and refrigerate some for the next day.

SERVES: 1
PREPARATION TIME: 10
NUTRITION: KCALS 504
NET CARBOHYDRATES 28G
FIBRE 13G
FAT 43G
PROTEIN 12G

INGREDIENTS:

♦ 1 Courgette

♦ 2 tbsp of Pine Nuts

♦ 2 tbsp of Fresh Basil

♦ 2 tsp of Oregano

♦ Half an Avocado

♦ 1 tbsp of Lime Juice

♦ 70ml of Water

♦ 5 Cherry Tomatoes

♦ Salt / Pepper to season

HOW TO PREPARE:

1 First, spiralize the courgettes to create your spaghetti and set it to one side.

2 Place the pine nuts, fresh basil, oregano, lime juice, water and half an avocado into a blender and blend at the highest speed.

3 Blend until the mixture is nice and smooth.

4 Pour the mixture over the courgette spaghetti and stir well.

5 Add the cherry tomatoes and season with salt and pepper to taste.

6 Serve up immediately or pack up and look forward to your delicious keto lunch.

STEAK, EGGS & AVOCADO

A Keto Lunch classic - Steak, Eggs, and Avocado. It's satisfying, comforting, and with food this tasty you'd never think you were on a "diet" at all. The important part of this meal is doing it how you like it; serve the eggs your favourite way, cook the steak how you like it, turn the avocado into guacamole if you really want to! It's your lunch - we've provided some inspiration below - but this comforting bowl is all about providing what you really want.

SERVES: 1
PREPARATION TIME: 15 MINS
NUTRITION: KCALS 923
NET CARBOHYDRATES 14G
FIBRE 7G
FAT 62G
PROTEIN 76G

INGREDIENTS:

- ♦ 2 Large Eggs
- ♦ Half an Avocado
- ♦ 200g of Flank Steak
- ♦ 1 tsp of Butter
- ♦ Soy Sauce
- ♦ Worcester Sauce
- ♦ Olive Oil
- ♦ Keto-Friendly Sweetener

HOW TO PREPARE:

1 Marinating your steak is not a necessity, but if you'd like to, make sure to do so at least an hour before cooking. You can use your favourite marinade, or combine a dash of soy sauce, keto-friendly sweetener, Worcester sauce, and a tablespoon of olive oil, and then coat the steak in the mixture.

2 Heat a non-stick pan and cook to the steak according to your tastes.

3 Once you have achieved your desired outcome, remove the steak from the pan and allow it to rest.

4 Take your avocado half and slice thinly, then set to one side.

5 Whisk your eggs in a small bowl and season with salt and pepper if desired.

6 Heat a pan over medium heat and then add the butter and allow it to melt.

7 Add the eggs to the pan and use a heatproof spatula to scramble them, allow to cook until firm.

8 Carefully tip the eggs out onto a plate. Take your steak and slice it into manageable sections, then add to the place with the eggs.

9 Finally, top your eggs with the fanned out avocado slices and season the plate with salt and pepper if desired.

BOX OF COLOUR

Simple, colourful, and completely customisable according to your tastes and cravings, preparing yourself a Box of Colour is preparing to eat the rainbow. The goal here is simple - eat as many different colours as you can. Doing so will help you hit your keto targets, fuel your body, and provide you with a plethora of nutrients and vitamins. So feel free to mix and match, change chicken for tuna, or swap cucumber and celery for spinach and kale, just make sure you're choosing lots of colours.

SERVES: 1
PREPARATION TIME: 15 MINS
NUTRITION: KCALS 675
NET CARBOHYDRATES 29G
FIBRE 7G
FAT 29G
PROTEIN 74G

INGREDIENTS:

- ◆ 1 Cooked Chicken Breast, sliced
- ◆ Tbsp of Mixed Nuts
- ◆ A handful of Cumber, sliced
- ◆ A handful of Celery, sliced
- ◆ 5 Cherry Tomatoes
- ◆ A handful of Red Onion, diced
- ◆ A handful of Red Berries and Blueberries
- ◆ 25g of Mature Cheddar, cubed
- ◆ 1 Large Egg, boiled

HOW TO PREPARE:

1   Get yourself a lunch box with at least three compartments, or indeed, get three small sealable containers.

2   Boil one large egg. (This can be done to taste but we recommend a firmer set yolk so that it can be halved and enjoyed with the salad.)

3   Slice your cooked chicken breast, cucumber, and celery, then dice your onion and cube your cheese

4   Halve your cherry tomatoes and boiled egg.

5   The savoury components will be fine in the same compartments, but we recommend storing the berries and nuts together in a separate section. You might also want to keep the chicken separate from the other elements while storing.

6   Make sure to refrigerate your meal to keep the ingredients cool, and then enjoy this quick little picnic box as soon as it's lunchtime!

PORK & CABBAGE STEW

It's healthy, hearty, and just the thing to warm you up on a cold afternoon. This incredibly tasty stew is easy to double up on quantities, so you can happily serve it up to the whole family knowing everyone is going to enjoy it. You can even refrigerate large quantities of the pork stew part and simply sauté the cabbage when you are ready to eat!

SERVES: 1
PREPARATION TIME: 1 HOUR
NUTRITION: KCALS 700
NET CARBOHYDRATES 24G
FIBRE 11G
FAT 57G
PROTEIN 30G

INGREDIENTS:

- 200g of Cauliflower Rice (Half a Cauliflower)
- 4 tsp of Coconut Oil
- 120g of Pork Shoulder
- 180g of Cabbage, shredded
- 120ml of Water
- 1 tbsp of Soy Sauce
- 2 tsp of Ground Ginger
- 1 Garlic Clove, crushed
- 1 tsp of Sesame Oil
- Salt / Pepper to taste
- 15g Mixed Sesame Seeds

HOW TO PREPARE:

1 First, place your cauliflower in a blender and process it until you achieve a light rice-like texture without any lumps or large pieces. Set to one side until required.

2 Cut the pork shoulder into manageable strips.

3 Heat a non-stick pan over medium to high heat and add 2 tsp of coconut oil. Allow the oil to melt, then add the pork and cook for 4 to 6 minutes until brown.

4 Add the garlic to the pan and allow it to cook for one minute.

5 Add the water, soy sauce, and ginger to the pan, and set the temperate to a level that allows to pan to simmer covered. Cook for approximately 40 minutes or until the pork is nice and tender.

6 While the pork mixture simmers, heat a non-stick pan over medium heat and add 1 tsp of coconut oil. Once the oil is coating the base of the pan, pour in your cauliflower rice and cook for about ten minutes, or until soft. Remove from pan and set in a small bowl ready to be served.

7 Take a small frying pan and over low heat gently toast your sesame seeds for a couple of minutes, being careful not to burn them. Then place on a plate to cool.

8 Using the pan that previously had the rice in, ensure it is clean before melting your remaining tsp of coconut oil.

9 Add the cabbage to the oil and cook until tender, then drizzle over the sesame oil and briefly stir before transferring the cabbage into a deep bowl.

10 After checking that the pork is good and tender, tip the pork and all of the liquid into the bowl with the cabbage. Sprinkle the bowl with your sesame seeds and serve alongside the cauliflower rice.

GREEK CHICKEN SALAD

Who doesn't love a Greek Chicken Salad? It is packed with healthy fats, low carb veggies, and will keep you in ketosis while allowing you to indulge in those satiating ingredients we all love to eat. This one couldn't be easier to prepare, so double up on quantities if you'd like to store some for tomorrow's lunch too!

SERVES: 1
PREPARATION TIME: 35 MINS
NUTRITION: KCALS 691
NET CARBOHYDRATES 38G
FIBRE 10G
FAT 31G
PROTEIN 68G

INGREDIENTS:

- 1 Chicken Breast
- 1 Courgette
- 2 tbsp of Olive Oil
- 5 Small Tomatoes
- Half a Red Onion
- 30g of Feta Cheese
- Pinch of Garlic Powder
- Pinch of Oregano
- Pinch of Parsley
- Splash of Balsamic Vinegar

HOW TO PREPARE:

1. First, pre-heat your oven to 200° Celsius.

2. Cut the courgette into cubes a couple of centimetres thick, then take the onion and cut it into four sections. Roughly separate the sections of onion so that approximately eight chunks remain together.

3. Halve the tomatoes, then place them in a mixing bowl along with the courgette cubes and onion.

4. Pour the olive oil into the mixing bowl along with the garlic powder, oregano, parsley, and a splash of balsamic vinegar. Stir the contents thoroughly to ensure everything is coated.

5. Tip the contents of the mixing bowl onto a baking tray and place in the oven for 25 minutes. You want the veggies to be soft (and lightly charred if desired) but not burnt.

6. Check on the vegetables halfway through cooking and stir to turn them slightly. Then return to the oven for the remainder of the cooking time.

7. While the vegetables are cooking, grill your chicken breast until cooked through and then slice it into bite-sized sections.

8. Once the vegetables are done, place them in a bowl and then crumble the feta cheese over them to garnish.

9. Place your chicken slices along the side of the bowl and serve with salt and pepper if desired.

PEANUT & COURGETTE NOODLES WITH CHICKEN

This is a perfect lunchtime meal to serve up to the entire family or to make and refrigerate for a week's worth of tasty keto lunches without any hassle or stress. You can easily moderate the spice level to your tastes, and the hearty courgette noodles will leave you feeling full and energised for the rest of the afternoon.

SERVES: 4
PREPARATION TIME: 40 MINS
NUTRITION: KCALS 650
NET CARBOHYDRATES 35G
FIBRE 13G
FAT 29G
PROTEIN 69G

INGREDIENTS:

- 4 Courgettes
- 4 Chicken Breast
- 4 tbsp of Sesame Oil
- 1 Head of Cabbage, roughly chopped
- 1 Red Pepper
- 1 Yellow Pepper
- 2 Spring Onions, finely chopped
- 70g of Organic Crunchy Peanut Butter
- 1 tbsp of Keto-Friendly Sweetener
- 100ml of Soy Sauce
- 3 Cloves of Garlic, chopped
- 2 tsp of Fresh Ginger, minced
- Pinch of Chilli Flaked (if desired)
- Splash of Asian Hot Sauce (if desired)

HOW TO PREPARE:

1. First, spiralize your courgettes, chop your cabbage, cut the peppers into thin strips, and then set all vegetables to one side.

2. Now chop your garlic cloves and mince your ginger ready to be used when required.

3. Chop your chicken into bite-sized chunks. Then heat a non-stick pan or wok over medium heat and add in one tablespoon of your sesame oil.

4. Cook your chicken until cooked through and nicely golden around the edges, then remove from the pan and place in a large bowl until needed.

5. Add two tablespoons worth of your sesame oil into the pan and allow to heat, then tip the cabbage and peppers into the pan and allow to cook for approximately 5 minutes or until they have reached your desired texture.

6. Then add your courgette noodles to the pan and stir, allowing them to be thoroughly coated with oil, and cook for 2 to 4 minutes until soft.

7. Remove all the vegetables from the pan and place them in the large bowl with the chicken.

8. Now add your remaining sesame oil to the pan, reduce the heat to a low setting, and cook the garlic in it for 1 minute. Then add the peanut butter, sweetener, soy sauce, ginger, and any spice elements you are using. Stir constantly until everything is combined and heated through - be careful not to burn it.

9. Tip the vegetables, courgette noodles, and chicken back into the pan with the peanut butter sauce and give everything a good stir. Make sure everything is well coated and nice and hot.

10. Serve with finely chopped spring onions to garnish and tuck into your healthy keto noodles!

DINNER

End your perfect Keto day with a hearty and nutritious meal that will satisfy your hunger and fuel your body until breakfast time. These tasty recipes are easy to modify so you can prepare them for yourself or serve them up for your friends and family to enjoy. Being on a diet should not mean that you have to miss out on evenings around the table with tasty food and good company, with these recipes you won't even have to prepare different dishes for your family, they will want to enjoy these dishes just as much as you do. The trick, as always, is to prepare your food to fit your lifestyle. So, if you know you are having a busy, do not plan to spend over an hour cooking something you will be too tired to enjoy. And you will also run the risk of snacking, and throwing yourself out of ketosis!

Instead, just as that busy day is beginning, throw together a slow cooker recipe and forget about having to cook until it is ready just when you need it to be.

AUBERGINE LASAGNE

You thought lasagne was a thing of the past? Think again! This tasty dish swaps the traditional pasta sheets for aubergine slices but doesn't compromise on any of the wonderful tomato and cheese flavour we associate with this Italian classic dish.

SERVES: 4
PREPARATION TIME: 40 MINUTES
NUTRITION: KCALS 517
NET CARBOHYDRATES 16G
FIBRE 6G
FAT 42G
PROTEIN 21G

INGREDIENTS:

- 1 Aubergine
- 1 tbsp of Olive Oil
- 1 Onion
- 2 Garlic Cloves
- 2 tbsp of Tomato Purée
- 200g of Chopped Tomatoes
- 100g of Ground Beef
- 1 tbsp of Oregano
- 1 tbsp of Basil
- 120g of Grated Cheese, plus extra for topping
- 200ml of Double Cream

HOW TO PREPARE:

1   First, pre-heat the oven to 200° Celsius.

2   Take the aubergine and very finely slice it lengthways, slices should be no more than half a centimetre in thickness. Place the slices on some kitchen towels to absorb moisture and set to one side.

3   Dice your onion and chop the garlic cloves. Then heat a non-stick pan over medium heat and add the olive oil. Once the oil is hot, add the garlic and onion to the pan and cook for a few minutes.

4   Tip the ground beef into the pan and cook until the mince is brown, then add the basil, oregano, tomato purée, and chopped tomatoes. Stir the mixture well then reduce heat and allow to simmer.

5   While the tomato and beef mixture is simmering, place a small pan over medium heat and add the double cream and cheese. Stir continuously so as not to allow the mixture to burn, and allow to simmer for 5 minutes.

6   Remove both sauces from the heat. In a large baking dish place one-third of the beef and tomato mixture in the base and then flatten so that it creates a layer. Then place a third of the aubergine slices over the mince.

7   Repeat the process until you have a three-layered lasagne, then top the final layer of aubergines with the cheese sauce, spreading it over the aubergines evenly. Then sprinkle your remaining cheese over the sauce to form the melted cheese top.

8   Bake in the oven for 20 minutes until the sauce is bubbling, then serve.

CREAMY LEMON SALMON & BROCCOLI

A perfectly balanced keto dish full of healthy fats and good sources of fibre, this meal should be a go-to recipe for anyone wanting to maintain their ketosis. Serve this salmon and delicious sauce with steamed tender stem broccoli and enjoy the dinner with your family and friends.

SERVES: 4
PREPARATION TIME: 15 MINUTES
NUTRITION: KCALS 545
NET CARBOHYDRATES 8G
FIBRE 3G
FAT 46G
PROTEIN 29G

INGREDIENTS:

- 4-5 Tender Stem Broccoli per person
- 85 Grams of Salmon Fillet per person
- 200ml of Vegetable Stock
- 240ml of Double Cream
- 40ml of Lemon Juice
- 4tbsp of Olive Oil
- 3 tbsp of Chives
- Salt / Pepper to taste

HOW TO PREPARE:

1 First, take the salmon portions from the fridge and allow them to come to room temperature while you prepare the sauce.

2 Create 200ml of vegetable stock with boiling water, then place it in a pan with the double cream, lemon juice, and chives, and cook over low heat. Whisk to combine and add salt and pepper to taste. Allow to gently simmer and thicken.

3 Steam the broccoli for a few minutes or until the desired texture is required, set aside, and keep warm until serving.

4 Heat the olive oil over a medium temperature in a non-stick pan, then add the salmon and allow to cook for approximately 4 minutes. Flip the salmon and allow 4 more minutes on the other side, until the salmon is golden on the edges and light pink in the middle.

5 Place the salmon onto the plate. Stir the lemon sauce and then pour it over each serving of salmon. Distribute the broccoli between the plates and serve immediately.

PULLED PORK & TOMATO

This spicy and comforting bowl of pulled pork with roast tomatoes, peppers, and slices of avocado is just the thing to finish off a long day and satisfy any cravings. The pork is easy to prepare and can be left in a slow cooker for 6 hours, so you can go about your day without worrying about it, and the roast veggies round out the meal with their nutrients and vitamins.

SERVES: 4
PREPARATION TIME: 6 HOURS FOR THE PORK ON LOW HEAT, PLUS 20 MINS PREPARATION TIME.
NUTRITION: KCALS 601
NET CARBOHYDRATES 21G
FIBRE 10G
FAT 44G
PROTEIN 33G

INGREDIENTS:

- 450g of Pork Shoulder
- 2 tsp of Smoked Paprika
- 3 tsp of Salt
- 2 tsp of Cajun Spice
- 1 tsp of Cayenne Pepper
- 1 tsp of Black Pepper
- 3 tbsp of Olive Oil
- 2 cloves of Garlic, crushed
- 1 tbsp of Red Wine Vinegar
- 1 Red Onion
- 1 Red Pepper
- 1 Yellow Pepper
- 5 Cherry Tomatoes per person
- Half an Avocado per person

HOW TO PREPARE:

1. First, mix the paprika, Cajun spice, cayenne pepper, black pepper, and 2 tsp of the salt into 2 tbsp of the olive oil.

2. Then rub the mixture into the pork shoulder until it is well coated. Place the pork into a slow cooker and cook on low heat for 6 hours.

3. When your pork had 30 minutes remaining, begin preparing your vegetables. Cut the red and yellow peppers into thin slices and place them in a mixing bowl with the cherry tomatoes.

4. Take the red onion and cut it into 8 to 20 chunks, operating some pieces so they are not too thick. Add the to the mixing bowl with the peppers and tomatoes.

5. Add the remaining tbsp of olive oil and the remaining tsp of salt to the mixing bowl, then add the tbsp of red wine vinegar. Mix well until everything is coated.

6. Place the coated vegetables on a baking tray and bake for 20 minutes.

7. While the vegetables are cooking take your avocados, halve them, and then cut them into thin slices. Then take each half and fan them out on a serving plate.

8. Remove the pork for the slow cooker and use forks to shred the meat apart.

9. Remove the vegetables from the oven and divide amongst the plates, then top each pile of vegetables with a scoop of pork shoulder.

10. Dig into your delicious pulled pork and roast vegetables!

SATAY BEEF

Scrumptious peanut sauce, flank steak, tender stem broccoli, green beans and sesame seeds, this recipe is so quick and easy it will quickly become a go-to evening meal. You can also try this recipe with cauliflower rice, or courgette noodles, or any low carb vegetables you desire. It also works perfectly as a lunchtime meal if you have any leftovers.

SERVES: 4
PREPARATION TIME: 15 MINUTES (PLUS ONE HOUR TO MARINATE)
NUTRITION: KCALS 589
NET CARBOHYDRATES 14G
FIBRE 5G
FAT 29G
PROTEIN 67G

INGREDIENTS:

- 200g of Flank Steak per person
- 200ml of Full Fat Coconut Milk
- 3 tbsp of Organic Peanut Butter
- 2 tbsp of Thai Red Curry Paste
- 1 tbsp of Lime Juice
- 1 tbsp of Soy Sauce
- 1 tsp of Keto-Friendly Sweetener
- 1 tbsp of Olive Oil
- 4-5 Tender Stem Broccoli per person
- A Handful of Green Beans per person

HOW TO PREPARE:

1 First, place the coconut milk, peanut butter, curry paste, lime juice, soy sauce, and sweetener into a bowl and whisk until all ingredients are combined.

2 Slice the beef steak into thin strips then add to the bowl with the peanut butter sauce, mix until everything is coated. Place the bowl in the fridge and allow it to marinate, you can do this for one hour, or prepare the mixture in the morning and allow it to marinate throughout the day for even more flavour.

3 Once marinated, cook the beef strips on a grill for a few minutes, turning each strip once. When they are cooked through, remove them from the grill and place them on a plate to rest. Keep them covered so they stay hot.

4 Heat the olive oil in a non-stick pan and then add in the tender stem broccoli and green beans, cook for 5 minutes or until they have achieved your desired texture.

5 Place the vegetables on serving plates and then top with the peanut butter beef strips and serve immediately for a tasty keto dinner everyone can enjoy!

KETO CHEESE BURGER

You thought you'd had your last cheeseburger? Think again! You don't need those stodgy carbs to make a delicious and satisfying cheeseburger that you'll want to serve up again and again. The trick to this dish is using the Gem Lettuce leaves like you would a shell, use one as the base and fill with the ingredients, and use the other to encase them and keep everything together.

SERVES: 1
PREPARATION TIME: 20 MINUTES
NUTRITION: KCALS 728
NET CARBOHYDRATES 17G
FIBRE 6G
FAT 52G
PROTEIN 47G

INGREDIENTS:

- 140g of Beef Mince
- 1 tsp of Smoked Paprika
- 1 tsp of Chipotle Paste
- 1 tsp of Tomato Paste
- 1 tbsp of Olive Oil
- 1 Garlic Clove, minced
- 30g of Cheddar Cheese
- 1 Beef Tomato
- 1 Dill Pickle
- 1 tbsp of Sour Cream
- 1 Head of Gem Lettuce

HOW TO PREPARE:

1. First, mince the garlic clove, and slice your tomato, cheese, and pickle into thin slices, then set to one side.

2. Heat the olive oil in a non-stick pan over medium heat, then add the beef mince and break apart with the spatula. Stir for a few minutes and then add the paprika, chipotle paste, tomato paste and minced garlic.

3. Stir all ingredients together and cook for 5 minutes or until the mince is cooked through.

4. Place one lettuce leaf on a plate facing upwards so that it acts like a cup, place a slice of tomato and a slice of cheese in the base, then scoop the mince onto the cheese until the lettuce cup is full.

5. Place a dollop of sour cream and the dill pickle on the top of the mince, then enclose with another lettuce leaf so that all the ingredients sit inside.

6. Repeat the process to create another lettuce cup full of ingredients and encase it with another lettuce leaf.

7. Enjoy your healthy keto cheeseburgers with all of the delicious flavours, but none of the heavy carbs!

BEEF & MUSHROOM STEW

Rich beef stew with low carb vegetables, just the thing to warm you through on a chilly evening and maintain your ketosis. This delicious and easily prepared stew is the perfect comfort dish and has all of the sump-tuous flavours you expect from a winter dish, without the heavy carbs.

SERVES: 4
PREPARATION TIME: 3 HOURS
NUTRITION: KCALS 675
NET CARBOHYDRATES 9G
FIBRE 2G
FAT 35G
PROTEIN 79G

INGREDIENTS:

♦ 1kg of Beef

♦ 1 Turnip

♦ 1 Onion

♦ 250g of Mushrooms

♦ 2 Celery Stalks

♦ 3 Cloves of Garlic

♦ 1 tbsp of Tomato Purée

♦ 3 tbsp of Olive Oil

♦ 1.5 litres of Beef Stock

♦ 2 tsp of Rosemary

HOW TO PREPARE:

1 First, cut the beef into chunky cubes and pat with kitchen towels to absorb moisture. Then coat the beef with 1 tbsp of olive oil.

2 In a large casserole dish or stove pot, heat a tsp of olive oil and then add the beef and allow it to brown slightly on each side. Then add the tomato purée and stir so that it coats the beef.

3 Add the beef stock and rosemary and then give everything a good stir. Allow the pot to simmer for between one and a half, and two hours. Check it is tender in the last half hour by inserting a fork.

4 During the last half hour of the beef cooking, chop the onion and turnip into chunks, and slice the celery into little half-moons. Then cut the mushrooms into bite-sized pieces.

5 In a small frying pan, heat the last of the olive oil and then cook the mushrooms for a few minutes.

6 If the beef is now tender, add the mushrooms, turnip, onions, and celery to the pot, then allow to simmer for up to an hour.

7 Once the vegetables are soft, but not overly done, turn off the heat and serve up your piping hot beef stew to the entire family. Season with salt and pepper according to taste.

CAULIFLOWER RICE & CHICKEN STIR FRY

This is a great one if you don't want to spend too much time standing over the oven preparing your evening meal. This stir fry is super quick, super easy, and super tasty! You can moderate the spice level by reducing the hot chilli sauce, or you can kick it up a notch by adding a little red chilli.

SERVES: 15
PREPARATION TIME: 1
NUTRITION: KCALS 543
NET CARBOHYDRATES 25G
FIBRE 9G
FAT 22G
PROTEIN 63G

INGREDIENTS:

- 1 Chicken Breast
- 2 tbsp of Sesame Oil
- 2 cloves of Garlic, crushed
- 4-5 Pieces of Tender Stem Broccoli
- Half a Red Pepper
- 200g of Riced Cauliflower
- 100ml of Chicken Stock
- A pinch of Sesame Seeds
- Half a Spring Onion, thinly chopped
- 2 tsp of Thai Style Chilli Sauce
- Half a tsp of Keto-Friendly Sweetener

HOW TO PREPARE:

1   Prepare your cauliflower rice by blending approximately half a floret until it takes on a rice-like texture with no lumps.

2   Cut your chicken breast into bite-sized pieces, then set to one side. Then slice your tender stem broccoli and red pepper into small pieces, and thinly chop the spring onion.

3   Crush your garlic cloves and set to one side, then made 100ml of Chicken Stock with boiling water.

4   Warm half of the oil in a non-stick pan and add the chicken pieces to it. Cook until they are golden on the outside and cooked through in the centre. Remove the chicken from the pan and set it to one side.

5   Heat the remainder of the oil in the pan, then briefly sauté the garlic. Now add the pepper and broccoli and cook until soft.

6   Add the chicken stock, chilli sauce, and sweetener, and give everything a good stir. Allow everything to cook for around 4 minutes.

7   Place the chicken pieces and cauliflower rice into the pan and mix together. Cook for another 4 minutes approximately, until the liquids have been absorbed and the cauliflower is soft but not oversaturated.

8   Transfer the stir fry into a bowl and garnish with spring onion and sesame seeds.

Olivia A. Parker

THE KETO 3 WEEK CHALLENGE

21 days of delicious meal plans to kickstart your ketogenic diet.

Each day you will find a bonus recipe to provide more variety and expand your repertoire.

Each day had been constructed to help you maintain ketosis, burn fat, and fuel your body.

But the beauty of this plan is that it is flexible!

You can swap out recipes that aren't to your taste with other recipes from the main body of the book, or you can repeat the things that you love to eat.

Or, even better, prepare big batches and eat throughout the week!

The next three weeks are all about showing you that a keto diet can fit around your lifestyle, so embrace the plan and face the challenges head-on!

DAY I

New Breakfast Recipe: Tomato Baked Eggs

Simple and delicious, this is a perfect Sunday morning treat that the whole family will want to dig in to. But, a little tip, if you don't want to share this breakfast will also keep well refrigerated for the next day. So seal it away and enjoy it as a cold breakfast or lunch later.

SERVES: 4
PREPARATION TIME: 1 HOUR
NUTRITION: KCALS 382
NET CARBOHYDRATES 12G
FIBRE 3.5G
FAT 29.5G
PROTEIN 17.75

INGREDIENTS:

- ◆ 8 Large Eggs
- ◆ 2 Red Peppers
- ◆ 800g of Cherry Tomatoes
- ◆ 4 cloves of Garlic
- ◆ 4 tbsp of Olive Oil
- ◆ 2 tbsp of Chopped Parsley
- ◆ Salt / Pepper to taste

HOW TO PREPARE:

1 Start by preheating your oven to 180° Celsius.

2 Chop your tomatoes into bite-sized chunks, thinly slice your peppers and crush the garlic.

3 Place all ingredients in a wide and shallow open proof dish, cover with olive oil and stir well.

4 Place the dish in the oven for approximately 40 minutes.

5 Remove the dish from the oven. Use a tablespoon to make 8 small gaps in the tomato mixture, and be careful as it will be very hot.

6 Break each egg into a gap, then cover the dish with foil to trap the heat.

7 Return the dish to the oven until the eggs have cooked to your desired level - just make sure all the egg white has set.

Lunch: Mushroom Risotto (See page 34)

Dinner: Aubergine Lasagne (See page 50)

DAY 2

Breakfast: Pancakes (See page 20)

New Lunch Recipe: Stuffed Avocados

Yum, the only possible way of making avocados better is stuffing them full of tasty treats. Remember you can use as little or as much of the spice as you'd like, it's your lunch!

SERVES: 4
PREPARATION TIME: 20 MINS
NUTRITION: KCALS 778
NET CARBOHYDRATES 30.2G
FIBRE 16.5G
FAT 64.5G
PROTEIN 27.25G

INGREDIENTS:

- 4 Avocados
- 1 tbsp of Olive Oil
- 350g of Beef Mince
- 1 Onion
- 4 cloves of Garlic
- 1 tsp of Cajun Spice
- 1 tsp of Smoked Paprika
- 1 tsp of Hot Chilli Spice
- 1 Lime
- 150g of Cherry Tomatoes
- A pinch of Salt
- 80g of Cheddar Cheese, grated
- 150g of Sour Cream
- 1 Head of Lettuce, roughly chopped

HOW TO PREPARE:

1 Chop your onion and crush the garlic.

2 Cut the tomatoes into quarters and slice the lime into wedges to serve on the side of the meal. Then roughly chop the lettuce into small strips.

3 Heat the olive oil in a large non-stick pan, place in the onions and allow to brown, then add the garlic and cook for a further minute.

4 Add the mince to the pan and break apart with a heatproof spatula. Season with Cajun spice, paprika, and salt. Stir occasionally while you complete the next step.

5 Cut each avocado in half and remove the stone. Then use a spoon to remove approximately a tablespoon's worth of avocado from each half. (You can keep what you have removed, cover it in lime juice, and eat it as guacamole the next day!)

6 Place each avocado bowl on a bed of lettuce.

7 Once the beef mince has cooked drain any excess liquid, and then fill each avocado bowl with beef, cheese, tomatoes, and top with sour cream.

Dinner: Beef Stew (See page 56)

DAY 3

Breakfast: Sausage, Egg & Avocado Tower (See page 24)

Lunch: Box of Colour (See page 40)

New Dinner Recipe: Goat Cheese Chicken & Mushrooms

A delicious and satisfying dinner that your friends and family will happily help you eat!

Pro tip: if you find your spinach has wilted down a lot you can always add more to bulk it back up.

SERVES: 4
PREPARATION TIME: 50 MINS
NUTRITION: KCALS 513
NET CARBOHYDRATES 9.25G
FIBRE 4G
FAT 22.25G
PROTEIN 66.75G

INGREDIENTS:

- ◆ 4 Large Chicken Breasts
- ◆ 400g of Spinach
- ◆ 3 tbsp of Olive Oil
- ◆ 3 Cloves of Garlic P
- ◆ 150g of Goats Cheese
- ◆ 1 Onion
- ◆ 750g of Chestnut Mushrooms
- ◆ 1 tsp of Basil
- ◆ 1 tsp of Thyme
- ◆ Salt / Pepper to taste

HOW TO PREPARE:

1 Start by preheating the oven to 190° Celsius.

2 Take each chicken breast and cut down the centre as if you were going to butterfly it, leave it connected on one side so you can open and close the top half.

3 Add 2 tbsp of olive oil to a large non-stick pan and warm over a medium temperature. Place the spinach inside the pan and stir as it begins to wilt.

4 Once wilted remove the spinach from the pan and place in a large bowl, then add the goat cheese. Stir so that all the ingredients combine. Then use a spoon to scoop a large dollop of the mixture into each chicken breast and enclose using the top half.

5 Leave the chicken to one side. Slice your mushrooms into thin slices, crush your garlic, and dice your onion.

6 Heat the remaining oil in the non-stick pan. Cook the onions until soft, then add the garlic and good for 1 minute. Then add the mushrooms, thyme, and basil. Cook until the mushrooms are browning.

7 Transfer the mushroom mixture into an ovenproof dish and spread it across the base. Add each chicken breast so that it nestles into its own bed of mushrooms. Over the dish with foil and bake in the oven for 30 minutes until the chicken is properly cooked.

8 Serve each chicken breast on its surrounding mushrooms, along with and cheese that may have escaped the chicken breast.

DAY 4

New Breakfast Recipe: Peanut Butter & Chocolate Smoothie

Quick and uncomplicated, this is a fantastic breakfast full of healthy fats that can be made in 2 minutes. So no excuses about how you didn't have time for breakfast, get to blending and go, go, go!

SERVES: 1
PREPARATION TIME: 2 MINS
NUTRITION: KCALS 878
NET CARBOHYDRATES 18G
FIBRE 14G
FAT 33G
PROTEIN 6G

INGREDIENTS:

- ◆ 1 Avocado
- ◆ 300ml Unsweetened Almond Milk
- ◆ 2 tbsp of Cacao Powder
- ◆ Half a tsp of Keto-Friendly Sweetener
- ◆ Water (to reduce thickness)
- ◆ Ice Cubes

HOW TO PREPARE:

1 Halve the avocado, remove the stone, and scoop the insides into a blender.

2 Add the cacao powder, almond milk, a drop of sweetener, and a few ice cubes.

3 Blend all the ingredients together. If the mixture becomes a bit too thick, add water as needed.

Lunch: Pork & Cabbage Stew (See page 42)

Dinner: Cauliflower Rice & Chicken Stir Fry (See page 62)

DAY 5

Breakfast: Green Eggs (See page 29)

New Lunch Recipe: Mushroom Soup

Now, you may be thinking there's no way you have time for making soup in the middle of the day! But that's where you're wrong. Not only is this soup quick and simple to make, but it also keeps really well in the fridge. So, cook up a big batch and keep it for a whole week of lunches!

SERVES: 4
PREPARATION TIME: 40 MINUTES
NUTRITION: KCALS 265
NET CARBOHYDRATES 7G
FIBRE 1.5G
FAT 26.75G
PROTEIN 3.25G

INGREDIENTS:

- ◆ 500g of Mushrooms
- ◆ 100g of Butter
- ◆ 1 Onion
- ◆ 3 cloves of Garlic
- ◆ 3 tbsp of Double Cream
- ◆ 1l of Chicken Stock

HOW TO PREPARE:

1. Dice the onions, crush the garlic, and slice the mushrooms.

2. Warm a large saucepan over medium heat and add the butter.

3. Add the onions to the pan and cook until soft and browning, then add the garlic and cook for a further minute.

4. Place the mushrooms in the pan and stir well to coat with butter. Cook for 5 minutes.

5. Make the chicken stock with boiling water and then add to the saucepan.

6. Allow the mixture to simmer for up to ten minutes.

7. Let the mixture cool slightly before attempting to blend. Be careful and make sure that the type of blender you are using can be used on hot liquids, and do not let it splash you.

8. Once blended place the mixture over low heat and begin stirring in the cream.

9. Serve when the soup is fully heated throughout.

Dinner: Keto Cheese Burger (See page 58)

DAY 6

Breakfast: Keto Granola (See page 22)

Lunch: Steak, Eggs & Avocado (See page 38)

New Dinner Recipe: Aubergine Stew with Feta

This is a perfect one for when you know you're about to have a busy day, but it's also great for just taking your foot off the accelerator for a bit and relaxing, because after a few simple minutes of prepping, this meal will be ready just when you want it to be.

SERVES: 4
PREPARATION TIME: 15 MINS PREP PLUS 7 HOURS IN A SLOW COOKER
NUTRITION: KCALS 456.75
NET CARBOHYDRATES 42.75G
FIBRE 17.75G
FAT 29.75G
PROTEIN 13.5

INGREDIENTS:

- 3 Aubergines
- 1 Red Onion
- 4 Clove of Garlic
- 6 tbsp of Olive Oil
- 250g of Cherry
- 1 Fennel Bulb
- 70g of Sundried Tomatoes
- 1 tsp of Coriander Seeds
- Basil Leaves, chopped
- Parsley Leaves, chopped

- 50 ml of Lemon Juice
- 150g of Feta Cheese

HOW TO PREPARE:

1. Chop the aubergine into slices of about 1cm in thickness, slice the fennel bulb, crush the garlic, cut the onion into thin strips, and halve the cherry tomatoes.

2. Put 4 tbsp worth of olive oil into a slow cooker, then place the onion and garlic at the bottom of the dish. Place each aubergine slice into the slow cooker, placing first one way, then the other, so both sides are coated with the oil.

3. Place the tomatoes, sun-dried tomatoes, and fennel slices amongst the aubergine, then sprinkle the coriander seeds over the dish. Leave in the slow cooker for 7 hours on low heat. Check if the aubergines are soft and if they are ready proceed to the next step.

4. Add the basil, parsley, lemon juice, and the remaining olive oil to a blender and process until well combined.

5. Arrange the aubergines and tomatoes on a plate. Finish the dish by drizzling over the salad dressing and crumbling the feta cheese onto the plate.

DAY 7

New Breakfast Recipe: Bacon & Spinach Frittata

This easy to make and scrumptious frittata is an indulgent breakfast that helps you forget you're on a diet at all. It is paired with a lighter lunch and fresh dinner so that your calories don't go wild, but you maintain ketosis.

SERVES: 4
PREPARATION TIME: 40 MINS
NUTRITION: KCALS 735.5
NET CARBOHYDRATES 4.75G
FIBRE 1.25G
FAT 65G
PROTEIN 33G

INGREDIENTS:

- ◆ 250g of Bacon Lardons
- ◆ 250g of Spinach
- ◆ 8 Large Eggs
- ◆ 2 tbsp of Butter
- ◆ 180 ml of Double Cream
- ◆ 100g of Cheddar Cheese

HOW TO PREPARE:

1   Preheat the oven to 180° Celsius and grate your cheese.

2   Use some of your butter to grease a large ovenproof dish or deep baking tray.

3   Heat a non-stick pan over medium heat and fry the bacon lardons in the rest of the butter.

4   Then add the spinach to the pan and briefly stir so that it is coated in the butter and has begun to wilt. Then tip the bacon and spinach into a bowl and set to one side.

5   Whisk the eggs in a bowl and then add the double cream and whisk again so that everything combines. Then pour the mixture into your greased baking dish.

6   Distribute the spinach on top of the egg mixture and then cover everything in a layer of grated cheese.

7   Bake for 30 minutes until golden and set.

Lunch: Avocado & Courgette Spaghetti (See page 36)

Dinner: Pulled Pork & Tomato (See page 54)

DAY 8

Breakfast: Berry & Avocado Smoothie (See page 28)

New Lunch Recipe: Tomato & Ricotta Salad

A simple and fresh salad that is easy to prepare and tasty to eat. You can even prepare this meal for future lunches and just withhold from putting it all together until you're ready to eat it.

SERVES: 4
PREPARATION TIME: 20 MINS
NUTRITION: KCALS 297.25
NET CARBOHYDRATES 23G
FIBRE 10.5G
FAT 19G
PROTEIN 14.25G

INGREDIENTS:

- 500g of Tomatoes (whatever variety you prefer)
- Half a Red Onion
- 100g of Mangetout
- 150g of Ricotta
- 3 sprigs of Tarragon
- 8 - 10 Basil Leaves
- 8 - 10 Parsley Leaves
- 1 tsp of Dijon Mustard
- 1 tbsp of Olive Oil
- 2 tsp of Red Wine Vinegar
- 2 Romain Lettuce Heads
- 70g of Almonds

HOW TO PREPARE:

1 First, prepare the dressing by finely chopping the basil and parsley. Then pick the leaves from the tarragon sprigs and add them to the other herbs.

2 Add the olive oil, mustard, and 1 tsp of the vinegar to the herbs and mix well. Taste the mixture and add more vinegar if you feel more acidity is required.

3 Cut the red onion into thin slices, slice the tomatoes into wedges, and diagonally halve the mangetout. Then roughly chop the lettuce.

4 Pile the salad ingredients on a plate and decorate with several dollops of ricotta per plate.

5 Dress the salad with the freshly prepared herb dressing, sprinkle with almonds, and serve immediately.

Dinner: Satay Beef (See page 56)

DAY 9

Breakfast: Raspberry & Vanilla Muffins (See page 26)

Lunch: Greek Chicken Salad (See page 44)

New Dinner Recipe: Sausage & Mushroom Frittata

Another tasty frittata, but with a new variety of flavours and textures to keep mealtimes exciting!

SERVES: 4
PREPARATION TIME: 20 MINS
NUTRITION: KCALS 462
NET CARBOHYDRATES 14.2G
FIBRE 2.5G
FAT 34.75G
PROTEIN 22.5G

INGREDIENTS:

- 300g of Chestnut Mushrooms
- 4 Pork Sausages
- 2 tbsp of Olive Oil
- 3 Cloves of Garlic
- 100g of Asparagus
- 100g of Tender Stem Broccoli
- 8 Large Eggs
- 4 tbsp of Sour Cream
- 2 tbsp of Wholegrain Mustard
- 2 tbsp of Tarragon, chopped

HOW TO PREPARE:

1 Start by removing the sausage meat from its skin and separating it into bite-sized chunks. Then crush the garlic, and quarter the mushrooms.

2 Heat the oil in a large, deep, non-stick pan, then fry the mushrooms for 4 minutes. Add the sausage meat and cook until they are cooked right through to the centre. Then add the garlic, asparagus, and broccoli, and cook for 2 more minutes.

3 Whisk the eggs in a bowl, then add the sour cream, mustard, and tarragon. Mix everything together well.

4 Pour the egg mixture into the pan allowing it to coat the sausage, asparagus, mushrooms, and broccoli. Cook over medium heat for 5 minutes.

5 Finish off the frittata by grilling for 2 minutes to set the top properly. Allow to cool for a minute and then divide and serve.

DAY 10

New Breakfast Recipe: Brussel Sprouts, Bacon & Baked Eggs

Ah sprouts, some people love them, some people slyly pass them to the dog at Christmas, but we beg you to try this tasty recipe that is certainly not just for Christmas.

SERVES: 4
PREPARATION TIME: 40 MINS
NUTRITION: KCALS 278.25
NET CARBOHYDRATES 9G
FIBRE 3.75G
FAT 16.5G
PROTEIN 20.5

INGREDIENTS:

- 10 - 12 strips of Streaky Bacon
- 8 Large Eggs
- 400g of Brussels Sprouts
- 3 Cloves of Garlic
- 1 Onion
- Salt / Pepper to taste

HOW TO PREPARE:

1 First, chop your spouts into bit-sized chunks, crush your garlic, and dice the onion.

2 Warm a large and deep stovetop pan over medium heat, then cook the bacon until your desired level of crispness.

3 Remove the bacon from the pan and set it on kitchen towels to absorb some of the grease.

4 Carefully wipe the excess bacon grease from the pan (carefully, it will be hot) and leave just enough on the bottom of the pan to cook your vegetables in.

5 Heat the remaining grease, then add the onions and sprouts and cook until onions are browned.

6 Add a few splashes of water to the pan and cook until the sprouts are tender, then add the garlic and cook for two more minutes.

7 Use a tablespoon to create 4 small gaps in the mixture, then break an egg into each space. Cover the pan with a lid and allow to cook until the egg whites have set and they have reached your desired firmness.

8 While the eggs are cooking, use scissors to cut your bacon into small pieces.

9 Once the eggs are done, scoop each portion out onto a plate. Top each egg with a handful of bacon bits and season with salt and pepper according to taste.

Lunch: Peanut & Courgette Noodles with Chicken (See page 46)

Dinner: Creamy Lemon Salmon & Broccoli (See page 52)

DAY 11

Breakfast: Sausage, Egg & Avocado Tower (See page 24)

New Lunch Recipe: Tuna & Daikon Salad

The mixture of textures and flavour makes this tuna and daikon salad one of the most interesting dishes, and it is packed full of satiating healthy fat. You will see that it is a lighter option to follow the calories heavy breakfast, but will still provide enough energy to see you through till dinner.

SERVES: 4
PREPARATION TIME: 40 MINS
NUTRITION: KCALS 271.75
NET CARBOHYDRATES 5.5G
FIBRE 1.25G
FAT 15.5
PROTEIN 29.25

INGREDIENTS:

- 2 tbsp of Sesame Oil
- 2 tbsp of Canola Oil
- 2 tbsp of Soy Sauce
- 50ml of Lemon Juice
- 1 Daikon
- Half a tsp of Keto-Friendly Sweetener
- 400g of Tuna Chunks, in water
- 200g of Bean Sprouts
- 1 tsp of Fresh Ginger, minced
- 1 Large Head of Napa Cabbage
- 1 tbsp of Coriander Leaves
- 1 tbsp of Sesame Seeds

HOW TO PREPARE:

1 Start by finely slicing the daikon, roughly chopping the cabbage, mincing the ginger, and chopping the coriander leaves.

2 Add the sesame oil, canola oil, soy sauce, lemon juice, and ginger into a small bowl and stir well.

3 Drain the tuna and place it in a large bowl. Add approximately a quarter of the dressing to the tuna and lightly stir.

4 Divide the cabbage, bean sprouts, and daikon amongst the plates. Add the tuna and garnish each plate with sesame seeds and coriander.

5 Serve with the dressing.

Dinner: Cauliflower Rice & Chicken Stir Fry (See page 62)

DAY 12

Breakfast: Spicy Egg Roll (See page 31)

Lunch: Mushroom Risotto (See page 34)

New Dinner Recipe: Chilli Con Carne

Who doesn't love a Chilli Con Carne? You certainly don't have to miss out on this classic Mexican dish just because you're on a diet.

SERVES: 4
PREPARATION TIME: 1 HOUR
NUTRITION: KCALS 535
NET CARBOHYDRATES 7.5G
FIBRE 1.25G
FAT 34.4G
PROTEIN 28.5G

INGREDIENTS:

- 1 Onion
- 500g of Beef Mince
- 3 cloves of Garlic
- 250ml of Beef Stock
- 1 tbsp of Tomato Purée
- 2 tsp of Chilli Powder
- 2 tsp of Cumin
- 2 tsp of Smoked Paprika
- Salt / Pepper to taste
- 1 can of Chopped Tomatoes
- 1 Red Chilli, deseeded and sliced (if required)

- 2 tbsp of Olive Oil
- 50g of Grated Cheese
- 100ml dollop of Sour Cream

HOW TO PREPARE:

1. Dice the onion, crush the garlic, and prepare the chilli if required.

2. Heat the olive oil in a large, deep, non-stick pan.

3. Add the onions to the pan and cook until soft. Then add the garlic and cook for 2 minutes.

4. Place the mince in the pan and use a heat-proof spatula to break apart, then add the cumin, chilli powder, paprika, and salt and pepper if required. You can also add the chilli now if you are using one.

5. Cook until the mince is browned.

6. Now add the chopped tomatoes and beef stock. Allow the mixture to simmer for 45 minutes, stirring occasionally.

7. Serve in bowls and top with a dollop of sour cream and sprinkle of cheese.

DAY 13

New Breakfast Recipe: Coconut Chia Bowl

Another great breakfast to prepare the night before, ideal for when you know you will be rushing out the door in the morning.

SERVES: 1
PREPARATION TIME: 2 MINS (PLUS OVERNIGHT SOAKING)
NUTRITION: KCALS 297
NET CARBOHYDRATES 23G
FIBRE 12G
FAT 19G
PROTEIN 11G

INGREDIENTS:

- 300ml of Coconut Milk
- 50ml of Water
- 40g of Chia Seeds
- 10g of Flaxseeds
- 50g of Berries
- Half a tsp of Keto-Friendly Sweetener

HOW TO PREPARE:

1 Place all of the ingredients in a bowl and mix well so that the berries break up.

2 Cover the bowl and refrigerate overnight so that all the liquids are absorbed.

3 When you're ready to eat your breakfast simply remove it from the fridge and dig in.

Lunch: Pork & Cabbage Stew (See page 42)

Dinner: Aubergine Lasagne (See page 50)

DAY 14

Breakfast: Pancakes (See page 20)

New Lunch Recipe: Aubergine Pizza

Pizza! With all of the good bits, and none of the stodgy carb-heavy base!

SERVES: 4
PREPARATION TIME: 50 MINS
NUTRITION: KCALS 252
NET CARBOHYDRATES 9.75G
FIBRE 2.5G
FAT 20G
PROTEIN 9G

INGREDIENTS:

- ◆ 3 Aubergines
- ◆ 4 tbsp of Olive Oil
- ◆ 4 cloves of Garlic
- ◆ 1 Onion
- ◆ 1 tbsp of Tomato Purée
- ◆ Half a can of Chopped Tomatoes (organic, no added sugar)
- ◆ 1 tsp of Basil
- ◆ 1 tsp of Oregano
- ◆ 1 tsp of Salt
- ◆ 40g of Parmesan Cheese
- ◆ 20g of grated Cheddar Cheese
- ◆ 30 g of Mozzarella Cheese

HOW TO PREPARE:

1. Preheat the oven to 180° Celsius.

2. Dice the onion, crush the garlic, and then slice the aubergines lengthways and of no more than one centimetre in thickness. Then take the mozzarella and cut it into thin slices.

3. Then place a large non-stick pan over medium heat and add 2 tbsp of oil. Cook the onions until soft and then add the garlic and cook for a further minute.

4. Add the tomato purée, chopped tomatoes, basil, oregano, and salt. Stir, and simmer until sauce thickens. Reduce to a low heat whilst completing the next steps.

5. Brush the slices of aubergine with the remaining olive oil, then grill them on both sides for a few minutes each.

6. Take two large baking trays and cover them with greaseproof paper. Lay each slice of aubergine onto the trays and cover the aubergine with slices of mozzarella. Then top each one with a small scoop of tomato sauce and spread it over the mozzarella. Then sprinkle the tomato sauce with parmesan and cheddar cheese.

7. Bake for 15 to 20 minutes or until all the cheese has melted and turned golden brown.

Dinner: Satay Beef (See page 56)

DAY 15

Breakfast: Berry & Avocado Smoothie (See page 28)

Lunch: Peanut & Courgette Noodles with Chicken (See page 46)

New Dinner Recipe: Chilli Salmon, Spinach & Asparagus

Salmon is one of the most keto-friendly ingredients you can have, and pairing it will the chilli and cheese makes for a sweet and creamy dish you'll want to make all the time.

SERVES: 4
PREPARATION TIME: 25 MINS
NUTRITION: KCALS 633
NET CARBOHYDRATES 23G
FIBRE 10G
FAT 41.25G
PROTEIN 44.25G

INGREDIENTS:

- ◆ 800g of Salmon Fillet
- ◆ 60g of Butter
- ◆ 120ml of Sour Cream
- ◆ 1 tbsp of Unsweetened Chilli Sauce
- ◆ 20g of Parmesan Cheese
- ◆ 450g of Spinach
- ◆ Salt / Pepper to taste

HOW TO PREPARE:

1. Preheat the oven to 180° Celsius. Then grease a large baking tray with 30g of butter.

2. Place the salmon in the baking tray skin side down.

3. Place the sour cream, cheese, and chilli sauce into a bowl and mix well. Then spread on top of each salmon fillet. Place in the oven and bake for around 20 minutes, or until the salmon is pale and flakes apart when touched.

4. When the salmon is almost done, heat a pan and melt the remaining butter, then add the spinach and sauté until it has wilted. Season with salt and pepper if desired.

5. Divide the salmon over the plates and then sit each salmon fillet atop its bed of spinach and serve immediately.

DAY 16

New Breakfast Recipe: Baked Mushroom & Eggs

It couldn't be simpler to prepare, and the flavours are just delicious. Don't be surprised if you find yourself using this as a lunch recipe too.

SERVES: 1
PREPARATION TIME: 25 MINS
NUTRITION: KCALS 390
NET CARBOHYDRATES 9G
FIBRE 3G
FAT 27G
PROTEIN 28G

INGREDIENTS:

- ◆ 2 Portobello Mushrooms
- ◆ 2 Large Eggs
- ◆ A handful of Grated Cheddar
- ◆ Salt / Pepper to taste
- ◆ A pinch of Chopped Parsley

HOW TO PREPARE:

1 Preheat the oven to 200° Celsius.

2 Line a baking tray with foil and remove the stalks from the mushrooms.

3 Place the mushrooms on the foil and bake for 10 – 12 minutes.

4 Remove the mushrooms from the oven and carefully crack an egg into each mushroom.

5 Bake until the egg has set and your desired firmness has almost been achieved.

6 Take the mushrooms out of the oven and sprinkle grated cheese over the egg, then return to the oven for one more minute.

7 Serve immediately with a pinch of chopped parsley.

Lunch: Greek Chicken Salad (See page 44)

Dinner: Keto Cheese Burger (See page 58)

DAY 17

Breakfast: Keto Granola (See page 22)

New Lunch Recipe: Shrimp Wraps

You don't need carb-heavy tortillas to enjoy shrimp wraps.

SERVES: 4
PREPARATION TIME: 20 MINS
NUTRITION: KCALS 363.5
NET CARBOHYDRATES 22.75G
FIBRE 12.255G
FAT 26.25
PROTEIN 14.25G

INGREDIENTS:

♦ 24 Large Shrimp

♦ 250g of Cherry Tomatoes

♦ Half a Red Onion

♦ 3 tbsp of Olive Oil

♦ 2 tbsp of White Wine Vinegar

♦ 1.5 Romain Lettuce Heads

♦ 1 tsp of Paprika

♦ A handful of Chopped Coriander

♦ 50ml of Lemon Juice

♦ 2 Avocados

♦ Salt / Pepper

HOW TO PREPARE:

1 Begin by halving the tomatoes and cutting the red onion into thin slices. Then separate the leaves of the lettuce and set to one side

2 Place 2 tbsp of olive oil, lemon juice, white wine vinegar, paprika, and any salt and pepper you require, into a small bowl. Whisk to combine.

3 Heat a non-stick pan over medium heat and add the remaining olive oil. Cook the shrimp until pink allowing approximately 2 minutes on either side. Then remove the shrimp from the pan and let them cool.

4 Halve the avocados and remove the stone, then remove the flesh from the skin cut it into cubes.

5 Place the tomato, red onion, coriander, avocado, and shrimp into a large mixing bowl and add the dressing. Give everything a good stir.

6 Place the lettuce leaves onto plates with their stalks all pointing inwards, so that they make a circle on the plate. Fill each lettuce leaf with a scoop of shrimp salad.

7 As you dig in, wrap each lettuce leaf around the shrimp salad to keep everything together.

Dinner: Pulled Pork & Tomato (See page 54)

DAY 18

Breakfast: Raspberry & Vanilla Muffins (See page 26)

Lunch: Avocado & Courgette Spaghetti (See page 36)

New Dinner Recipe: Butter Chicken & Cauliflower Rice

This recipe is worth that extra bit of time and care, it's so moreish we are sure you'll be making it again and again.

SERVES: 4
PREPARATION TIME: 50 MINS
NUTRITION: KCALS 571.25
NET CARBOHYDRATES 11.25G
FIBRE 1.25G
FAT 31.5G
PROTEIN 59G

INGREDIENTS:

- 1 Cauliflower Head
- 4 Chicken Breasts
- 3 tbsp of Garam Masala
- 5 cloves of Garlic
- 1 Onion
- 2 tbsp of Ghee
- 100g of Plain Full Fat Yoghurt
- 2 tbsp of Coconut Oil
- Half a tbsp of Olive Oil
- 1 can of Chopped Tomatoes
- 1 tbsp of Ground Coriander
- 3 tsp of Cumin
- 1 tsp of Chilli Powder
- 100ml of Double Cream
- 150ml of Water

HOW TO PREPARE:

1 Slice the chicken breasts into thin strips and place them in a mixing bowl. Then crush your garlic and dice your onions. Then blend the cauliflower head into cauliflower rice and set aside.

2 Add 2 tbsp of garam masala, half of the crushed garlic, and the yoghurt. Mix well, then cover and refrigerate for 30 minutes.

3 While the chicken marinates, warm a large, deep, pan over medium heat, and add half the coconut oil. Cook the onions until they become soft and clear, then add the remaining garlic. Cook for 2 more minutes.

4 Add the chopped tomatoes, cumin, chilli powder, ground coriander and the remaining tbsp of garam masala. Before the contents warm up, blend well with a hand blender until smooth, then set to simmer.

5 While the sauce cooks, remove the chicken from the fridge. Heat a non-stick pan and warm the remaining coconut oil. Place the chicken strips in the pan and allow to cook for 4 minutes per side. Then remove the chicken from the pan and place it in the sauce. Turn up the heat slightly and cook for around 5 minutes.

6 While the curry is cooking, heat the olive oil in the saucepan and pour in the cauliflower rice. Cook for a minute before adding the water and cooking until soft. Once cooked, remove from pan and place in serving bowls.

7 Return to the curry pan. Stir in the ghee and double cream and cook for 2 minutes.

8 Remove the pan from the heat and scoop servings of the curry on top of the cauliflower rice to serve.

DAY 19

New Breakfast Recipe: Avocado Bowls

You know the drill by now, hollow them out, fill them with tasty treats!

SERVES:1
PREPARATION TIME: 20 MINS
NUTRITION: KCALS 532
NET CARBOHYDRATES 17G
FIBRE 14G
FAT 49G
PROTEIN 12G

INGREDIENTS:

♦ 1 Avocado

♦ 4 strips of Streaky Bacon

♦ 1 tbsp of Butter

♦ Salt / Pepper to taste

HOW TO PREPARE:

1 Start by halving your avocado and removing the stone. Then scoop out about a tablespoon's worth of avocado from the centre – you want to be left with enough space to put your scrambles eggs, but it should not be so deep as to be close to the skin.

2 Place any avocado you have removed from each half in the fridge with a dash of lime juice, you can use it for your Lunch Box of Colour later if you'd like.

3 Heat a non-stick pan and begin to fry your bacon until the desired level of crispness, then set to one side and pat with kitchen paper to soak up some of the grease.

4 Take a pair of scissors and cut the bacon into little pieces.

5 Heat a non-stick pan and melt the tbsp of butter. While the butter is melting crack your eggs into a bowl and whisk.

6 Add the eggs into the melted butter and begin to scramble. As the eggs begin to firm add in your bacon bits and stir.

7 Remove the pan from the heat and scoop the bacon and egg mixture into your avocado bowls.

Lunch: Box of Colour (See page 40)

Dinner: Beef & Mushroom Stew (See page 60)

DAY 20

Breakfast: Spicy Egg Roll (See page 31)

New Lunch Recipe: Cauliflower Salad

Well, it's not so much a salad as it is a combination of scrumptious ingredients that work wonderfully well together.

SERVES: 4
PREPARATION TIME: 15 MINS
NUTRITION: KCALS 291.25
NET CARBOHYDRATES 3G
FIBRE N/A
FAT 24.5G
PROTEIN 14G

INGREDIENTS:

♦ 1 Cauliflower Head, separated into florets

♦ 8 slices of Streaky Bacon

♦ 200g of Sour Cream

♦ 100g of Grated Cheddar Cheese

♦ 1 tbsp of Lemon Juice

♦ 2 tbsp of Chopped Chives

♦ 1 tsp of Garlic Powder

♦ Salt / Pepper to taste

HOW TO PREPARE:

1 Bring a large pan of water to boil and add in your cauliflower florets. Cook for 5 minutes, then drain and set to one side.

2 Heat a non-stick pan over medium heat and cook the bacon until your desired level of crispness has been achieved. Then remove from the pan and place on kitchen towels to soak up excess grease.

3 While the cauliflower and bacon are cooling, mix the sour cream, lemon juice, garlic powder, and salt and pepper in a large bowl.

4 Cut the bacon into small pieces and add it to the mixing bowl. Then add the cauliflower and cheese and gently stir everything together.

5 Separate into bowls and garnish each with chopped chives.

Dinner: Creamy Lemon Salmon & Broccoli (See page 52)

DAY 21

Breakfast: Green Eggs (See page 29)

Lunch: Steak, Eggs & Avocado (See page 38)

New Dinner Recipe: Chicken & Tomato Courgette Noodle

Courgette Noodles are the ultimate carb replacement, they are versatile, delicious, and work fantastically in this dinner dish.

SERVES: 4
PREPARATION TIME: 20 MINS
NUTRITION: KCALS 512
NET CARBOHYDRATES 23.5G
FIBRE 4.75G
FAT 25G
PROTEIN 49.5G

INGREDIENTS:

- ◆ 3 tbsp of Olive Oil
- ◆ 1 Onion
- ◆ 3 Chicken Breast
- ◆ 3 Cloves of Garlic
- ◆ 3 Courgettes
- ◆ 1 can of Chopped Tomatoes
- ◆ 16 Cherry Tomatoes
- ◆ 100g of Cashew Nuts
- ◆ 1 tsp of Basil
- ◆ 1 tsp Oregano
- ◆ Salt / Pepper to taste

HOW TO PREPARE:

1 Cut the chicken into bite-sized chunks, dice the onion, halve the cherry tomatoes, crush the garlic, and spiralize the courgettes.

2 Heat the oil in a non-stick pan, then add the onion and cook until soft and browning. Add the garlic, cook for a minute, then add the chicken pieces and stir. Season with oregano, basil, and salt and pepper, then cook for 5 minutes.

3 Once the chicken is golden, add the chopped tomatoes and let simmer for a few minutes.

4 Whilst the chicken pan is simmering, toast the cashews in a small pan until golden brown, then remove from the heat.

5 Add the courgette noodles to the tomato and chicken sauce, and then stir in the cherry tomatoes. Cook for 2 minutes.

6 Serve into bowls and top with toasted cashew nuts.

DISCLAIMER

This book contains opinions and ideas of the author and is meant to teach the reader informative and helpful knowledge while due care should be taken by the user in the application of the information provided. The instructions and strategies are possibly not right for every reader and there is no guarantee that they work for everyone. Using this book and implementing the information/ recipes therein contained is explicitly your own responsibility and risk. This work with all its contents, does not guarantee correctness, completion, quality or correctness of the provided information. Misinformation or misprints cannot be completely eliminated.

Printed in Great Britain
by Amazon

75384694R00066